Math Counts

Time

Introduction

In keeping with the major goals of the National Council of Teachers of Mathematics Curriculum and Evaluation Standards, children will become mathematical problem solvers, learn to communicate mathematically, and learn to reason mathematically by using the series Math Counts.

Pattern, Shape, and *Size* may be investigated first—in any sequence.

Sorting, Counting, and *Numbers* may be used next, followed by *Time, Length, Weight,* and *Capacity.*

Ramona G. Choos, Professor of Mathematics, Senior Adviser to the Dean of Continuing Education, Chicago State University; Sponsor for Chicago Elementary Teachers' Mathematics Club

About this Book

Mathematics is a part of a child's world. It is not only interpreting numbers or mastering tricks of addition or multiplication. Mathematics is about *ideas*. These ideas have been developed to explain particular qualities such as size, weight, and height, as well as relationships and comparisons. Yet all too often the important part that an understanding of mathematics will play in a child's development is forgotten or ignored.

Most adults can solve simple mathematical tasks without the need for counters, beads, or fingers. Young children find such abstractions almost impossible to master. They need to see, talk, touch, and experiment.

The photographs and text in these books have been chosen to encourage talk about topics that are essentially mathematical. By talking, the young reader can explore some of the central concepts that support mathematics. It is on an understanding of these concepts that a child's future mastery of mathematics will be built.

Henry Pluckrose

1995 Childrens Press® Edition
© 1994 Watts Books, London, New York, Sydney
All rights reserved.
Printed in the United States of America.
Published simultaneously in Canada.
1 2 3 4 5 6 7 8 9 0 R 04 03 02 01 00 99 98 97 96 95

Math Counts

Time

By Henry Pluckrose

Mathematics Consultant: Ramona G. Choos,
Professor of Mathematics

CHILDRENS PRESS®
CHICAGO

What do we mean by *time*?
Time is a measure of the hours,
days, months, and years
we live through.

4

What time do you go to school, have lunch, and go to bed?

5

We measure time so we can keep
track of events.
We need to know what time
a bus will come

6

and what time a train will leave the station.

We need to measure moments of time
to know how long things take.
How long does it take to boil
an egg so the yolk looks like this?

8

How do you make sure
that toast does not burn?

9

We measure each day
in hours from midnight.
There are 12 hours
from midnight to midday,

and 12 hours from midday
to midnight.
There are 24 hours
in a whole day.

Clocks measure time.
A clock has 2 hands.
The long hand marks the minutes.
The short hand marks the hours.

It takes 60 minutes for the long hand
to go around the clock face.
There are 60 minutes in each hour.

This is a digital watch.
Which number shows the hours?
Which number shows the minutes?

We measure short periods of time in seconds.
A special kind of watch is used to time a race.
The big hand measures seconds.
The small hand measures minutes.

The watch is started when the race begins. The watch is stopped when the winner crosses the finish line.

15

Longer periods of time
are measured in weeks.
Seven days make one week.
On which day does
the school week begin?

16

GREEN
Beans
98¢ lb

Baking Potatoes
39¢

GARLIC
$2.29

WAX BEANS
$1.29

On which days do most people do their week's shopping?

A month is a longer period
of time than a week.
Some months last for 30 days
and some last for 31 days.
How is February different?
Winter months often are cold.

Summer months often are hot.
Some people go on vacation
near the ocean.

Twelve months make one year.
On your first birthday,
you celebrated one year of life.

Everyone has birthdays.
This lady is enjoying a party
to celebrate her birthday.

21

We measure our age in years.
How old is the child
who will have this cake?

22

We mark the passing of time
in many other ways—
by celebrating special holidays,
such as New Year's Day,

by wearing special clothes,

or by watching fireworks.

Before people invented clocks,
they measured time
with shadows

and even with candles.

27

Départs   Departures

Horaire / Schedule	Destination / Destination	Vol / Flight	Satellite / Satellite	Observation / Remarks
1:00	LONDON-H	BE 9357	••	TERMINE DEPARTED
7:50	MANCHEST	AF 960.6	••	EMBARQUEMENT BOARDING
8:00	LONDON-G	BR 881.3	••	EMBARQUEMENT BOARDING
8:00	LONDON-H	AF 842.6	••	EMBARQUEMENT BOARDING
8:10	MUNICH	AF 730.4	••	EMBARQUEMENT BOARDING
8:10	BRAZZA	UT 777.7	••	EMBARQUEMENT BOARDING
8:15	BERLIN W	AF 760.5	••	EMBARQUEMENT BOARDING
8:15	DUSSELDF	AF 760.5	••	
8:30	ROME	AF 632.6	••	EMBARQUEMENT BOARDING
8:30	PEKIN	CA 932.4	••	EMBARQUEMENT BOARDING
8:30	MRSEILLE	IT 021.7	••	EMBARQUEMENT BOARDING
8:30	LE-CAIRE	TW 800.2	••	EMBARQUEMENT BOARDING
8:30	COPENHAG	SK 560.3	••	EMBARQUEMENT BOARDING
8:50	NICE	AF 070.7	••	
9:00	LONDON-H	AF 844.6	••	

Horaire / Schedule	Destination / Destination	Vol / Flight	Satellite / Satellite	Observation / Remarks
9:00	MANCHEST	AF 4670	••	ANNULE CANCELLED
9:00	LYON	IT 011.7	••	EMBARQUEMENT BOARDING
9:00	MOSCOU	SU 254.4	••	EMBARQUEMENT BOARDING
9:00	OUAGA	UT 8267.1	••	EMBARQUEMENT BOARDING
9:10	OSLO	AF 796.4	••	
9:20	HELSINKI	AF 790.4	••	
9:30	LONDON-G	BR 883.3	••	
9:30	JEDDAH	AF 124.4	••	
9:35	TOULOUSE	IT 039.7	••	
9:35	TOKYO	JL 464.2	••	
9:40	DUBAI	AF 152.6	••	
9:45	BRUSSELS	AF 642.5	••	
9:45	AMSTERDM	KL 324.3	••	
9:45	RYAD	SV 770.3	••	
9:55	MOSCOU	SU 318.4	••	

Départs   Departures

8 00

But a moving shadow or a burning candle
does not give an exact measure
of passing time.
Planes have to fly to a timetable.

28

To catch a plane you need to be at the airport on time.
Otherwise the plane will take off without you.

There always has been time.
This castle was built
many hundreds of years ago.
It is now a ruin.

This skyscraper was built recently. Long ago, even the castle was new and modern.

Library of Congress Cataloging-in-Publication Data

Pluckrose, Henry Arthur.
    time / Henry Pluckrose.
      p. cm.
    Originally published: London; New York: F. Watts, 1988.
    (Math counts)
    Includes index.
    ISBN 0-516-05459-7
    1. Time — Juvenile literature. [1. Time.] I. Title.
QB209.5.P58 1995
529 — dc20
                                        94-38011
                                        CIP
                                        AC

Photographic credits: Chris Fairclough, 4, 6, 7, 8, 9, 10, 11, 12, 13, 14, 15, 16, 17, 18, 22, 24, 25, 26, 27, 29, 30, 31; Unicorn Stock Photos, © Tommy Dodson, 5, 21; © John Ward, 19; © Jean Higgins, 20; ZEFA, 24; © Adam Woolfitt, 23; Robert Harding Picture Library, 28

Editor: Ruth Thomson
Assistant Editor: Annabel Martin
Design: Chloë Cheesman

INDEX